AI in the Automotive Industry

Transforming Cars and Transportation

Table of Contents

Chapter 1. Introduction

In our Special Report, titled "AI in the Automotive Industry: Transforming Cars and Transportation", we illuminate the pivotal role that artificial intelligence plays in remolding the car industry. It is not a realm of sci-fi but tangible advancements that we are witnessing today. We delve into how AI is being integrated into cars and transforming transportation, spanning from smart navigation systems to autonomous vehicles. This vital report is not laden with overly complex technical jargon but relates this innovative shift in a clear, comprehensible manner. Regardless of whether you're an industry insider, an enthusiastic technophile, or simply an everyday car user interested about the future of your driving experience, this report offers insightful knowledge illustrating why AI adoption is a route the automotive world is determined to follow. Purchase this Special Report today to gain an in-depth understanding of this exciting juncture where technology meets transportation.

Chapter 2. Unfolding the Connection: Artificial Intelligence and Automobiles

Artificial Intelligence (AI) has been making waves in various industries, radically transforming traditional methods of operation. Among these, the automobile industry represents an especially vibrant arena for AI implementation. The connection between AI and automobiles is not merely a fanciful vision of the future, but a lived reality that's unfolding with each passing day. Let's take an in-depth look at how this connection is reshaping the automotive landscape and propelling us towards a new era of intelligent transportation.

2.1. How AI Came on Board

AI stepped into the automobile industry through small, incremental advancements initially. AI-based features such as voice-activated controls, automatic parking, driver assist systems, and GPS navigators marked the beginning of a transformative journey. We began to witness the increasing incorporation of AI-enabled features in our vehicles, instigating a shift from traditional mechanical functionalities to more advanced, adaptive, and intelligent functions. This marked the inception of AI's deep-seated relationship with the automobile industry.

2.2. Under the Hood: Understanding AI's Role in Today's Cars

AI today is not just a fancy add-on but a decisive force in the car's operation. What was introduced as a driver-assist feature has evolved into managing central functions in a car's working. Be it fuel management, navigation, vehicle maintenance, or security, AI dons multiple hats within a vehicle's ecosystem.

For instance, vehicle diagnostics and preventive maintenance, handled traditionally by human eyes and hands, is now being delegated to AI. A series of sensors embedded within the car can diagnose critical vehicle components for potential faults, alert the user and prompt preventive maintenance.

AI-driven cybersecurity in cars is another significant advancement. With vehicles becoming more connected, they are also becoming more prone to cyberattacks. AI steps in here, offering machine learning algorithms that predict, detect, and mitigate potential threats.

2.3. Moving Towards Autonomy: AI and Self-Driving Cars

Perhaps the most thrilling proposition is the advent of autonomous, or self-driving vehicles, which fully embody the integration of AI in the automotive world. Often seen as the zenith of AI application in the automobile industry, these autonomous vehicles rely on AI for nearly all their functions. Dozens of sensors, radars, and cameras give these vehicles a 360-degree view of their surroundings, and AI processes this data in real-time to navigate roads, avoid obstacles, and make driving decisions.

These vehicles learn from their experiences, mimicking human drivers' instinctive responses, but without human shortcomings of fatigue or distraction. While full autonomy is still being rigorously tested and refined, the presence of semi-autonomous cars on our roads is a testament to the transformative power of AI.

2.4. Ethical and Regulatory Challenges

While discussing AI's integration in automobiles, it's crucial to acknowledge the accompanying ethical and regulatory challenges. As AI assumes control, the question of accountability arises. Who is responsible in case of an AI's misjudgment leading to an accident? How do we ensure the AI's decision-making aligns with human expectations of safety and ethics?

Policymakers worldwide grapple with these questions as they attempt to create regulation that can keep pace with technological advancements. Standardized testing methodologies, elaborate data protection regulations, and predefined guidelines for AI behavior are some approaches currently under review.

2.5. A Look Into the Future

As we look to the horizon, it's clear that AI is set to profoundly transform our transportation experience. Future advancements promise AI-managed traffics, where intelligent systems could regulate traffic flow, reduce congestion and improve overall road safety.

Furthermore, concepts like AI-driven vehicle-to-vehicle (V2V) and vehicle-to-infrastructure (V2I) communication systems paint a picture of seamless coordination among vehicles and infrastructure. This harmonious interplay can drastically reduce the incidence of road accidents, optimizing our driving experience and reshaping our urban spaces.

Unfolding the connection between AI and automobiles reveals an engagement that has evolved from mere convenience to becoming a central player. As AI continues to redefine limits, the marriage between artificial intelligence and the automobile industry offers a glimpse of the extraordinary future of transportation.

Chapter 3. The Drive Towards Smart Navigation Systems

As the digital revolution continues to impact every sector of the economy, artificial intelligence is carving a pivotal role in the automotive industry. AI is not just an auxiliary tool in this revolution, but the driving force behind the emergence of smart navigation systems in cars today. The integration of AI with navigation systems is creating a safer, more efficient driving experience for everyone on the road.

3.1. The Paradigm Shift from Traditional Navigation Systems to AI-driven Systems

Navigating through unfamiliar territory was once a challenging endeavor that often resulted in getting lost, causing unnecessary detractions from travel plans. GPS technology changed that, and in turn, became the cornerstone of modern navigation systems.

However, current demands for complexity and real-time data processing surpass the capabilities of legacy GPS technology. These propel the advent of AI-driven smart navigation.

AI-powered smart navigation systems not only provide real-time traffic updates, but also cultivate personalized recommendations based on driver habits and preferences, demonstrating a significant paradigm shift.

3.2. The Core components of AI-Driven Smart Navigation Systems

AI-driven navigation systems comprise a synergy of technologies, where each has a vital role in providing a seamless driving experience.

Machine Learning - Machine learning algorithms have the capacity to learn from data without explicit programming. They analyze large datasets to predict traffic patterns and suggest optimal routes, adjusting in real-time to changes in traffic flow.

Big Data Analysis - AI harnesses vast amounts of data generated from various sources such as satellites, traffic cameras, and other vehicles. These are processed to provide accurate, real-time traffic updates and directions to the driver.

Internet of Things - With GPS, cameras, sensors, and internet connectivity, AI can gather data, analyze it, and communicate the results to the driver.

3.3. Personalized Driving Experience through AI

One of the standout properties of AI-driven smart navigation is its ability to deliver personalized experiences. By analysing driver habits and preferences, systems can create custom routes to frequently visited locations, account for personal speed preferences, and even suggest preferable times for travel.

Machine learning models integrated within these systems learn from every journey, storing data such as routes and driver behaviors. This data repository generates a more personal experience, making navigation both familiar and comfortable to the driver.

3.4. Enhancing Safety with AI Navigation

AI-powered navigation systems perform several functions to enhance driver safety. The systems observe the driver's speed, location, and other extenuating circumstances to suggest the safest route home.

Moreover, AI camera systems provide a 360-degree view of the vehicle's surroundings, alerting the driver to potential hazards. In some advanced models, predictive capabilities can anticipate potential incidents, suggesting preventative measures.

3.5. Future Advancements: Augmented Reality in Navigation

Looking ahead, augmented reality (AR) promises to add another dimension to how we navigate. By overlaying navigation information on a display showing the real world, AR can lead to more intuitive and safer navigation.

Despite being a nascent technology, it holds great promise. As AI continues to develop, it is poised to make AR navigation a standard feature in vehicles, turning a once-abstract dream into a tangible reality.

3.6. Concluding Remarks

Emerging from the chrysalis of nascent technology, AI has found its way into every corner of life, emblazoning its mark on the automotive industry's navigation systems. Today, the advent of AI-driven navigation technologies is transforming the driver experience.

As AI matures and embraces new tools like AR, the automotive industry stays poised to offer even more nuanced and immersive experiences to drivers. But no matter what the future holds, the focus remains, as it should, on creating a safer, more efficient, and enjoyable driving experience.

This is a breakthrough that couldn't have come at a better time. As the world moves forward, AI propels us alongside it - and nowhere is this reality more perceptible than within the car industry.

Chapter 4. Automatic and Assisted Driving: AI at the Wheel

Typically seen as the domain of science fiction, the advent of artificial intelligence (AI) in the automotive industry is now a reality we cannot afford to overlook. Advances in AI technology and machine learning algorithms have paved the way for critical developments in automatic and assisted driving systems. These systems are swiftly being integrated into our vehicles, improving the way we navigate, and potentially revolutionizing our entire perception of transportation.

4.1. Introduction

Assisted driving aids and complete automation are a couple of the broad categories into which AI-powered technologies in vehicles fall. At one end of the spectrum, we have systems that assist drivers with performing specific tasks like parking assistance and lane departure warning. At the other end, we have autonomous vehicles (AVs) capable of navigating roads with no human intervention. While still in its infancy, this burgeoning field has promising potential to transform transportation by improving road safety, enhancing driving experiences, and shaping new mobility systems.

4.2. Assisted Driving Systems

In recent years, Assisted Driving Systems (ADS), which blend human control with machine guidance, have grown in popularity. These technologies do not replace human involvement in driving but rather enhance and buttress it, providing alerts, warnings, and limited vehicle control.

Automatic Emergency Braking (AEB) stands as one prime example. This system assists the driver by automatically applying the brakes when an impending frontal collision is detected, minimizing potential damage or avoiding the accident altogether.

Similarly, Lane Keeping Assists (LKA) and Lane Departure Warnings (LDW) serve to protect the driver and vehicle from drifting out of lane unintentionally. Here, AI algorithms are used to analyze camera inputs, detect lane markings, and apply corrective measures to assist the driver.

Another significant function of ADS is Adaptive Cruise Control (ACC), a technology that automatically adjusts the vehicle's speed to maintain a predetermined distance from the car in front. AI algorithms monitor the leading vehicle and traffic conditions to modulate the car's speed appropriately.

4.3. Evolution Towards Full Automation

While assisted driving technologies enhance the overall driving experience, the bigger revolution lies in fully automated vehicles. AI's role is far more crucial here, as it extends beyond the realm of assistance to full control of a vehicle.

This shift towards full automation is typically outlined in six levels (0 to 5) according to SAE International's classification. Level 0 refers to no automation, and level 5 refers to complete automation involving AI technology that governs all driving tasks in all conditions.

As of now, the industry is generally operating around the level 2 and 3, where the vehicle can take over specific functions such as steering, accelerating, and braking but require human intervention when the system cannot respond.

Vehicles operating at level 4 and 5 are known as Autonomous Vehicles (AVs), where human drivers are not necessary. The vehicle can perform all driving functions under certain conditions (level 4) or in all conditions (level 5).

4.4. Technical Framework of Autonomous Vehicles

Autonomous vehicles captivate our imagination, often sparking visions of futuristic landscapes. However, achieving this vision is a formidable technical challenge. AVs are expected to safely navigate complex, ever-changing environments, reacting appropriately in any situation. This requires a sophisticated blend of sensors, computational hardware, and advanced AI.

The sensors, such as cameras, LIDAR, RADAR, and ultrasonic devices, collect data from the surrounding environment. This information is processed by high-performance computing hardware running AI algorithms to perceive the environment, plan the path, and control the vehicle's movements.

Object detection and recognition are key tasks performed by AV's perception system. AI models identify other vehicles, pedestrians, cyclists, traffic signs, and various other elements in the environment. The relative positions, dimensions, and velocities of these objects are determined, helping the vehicle to plan its path.

The high-level decision-making within an AV is performed by the planning system. Using the perception system's output, it computes the vehicle's upcoming trajectory, deciding when to speed up, slow down, overtake, or make a turn.

Finally, control algorithms take the planned trajectory and translate it into actionable commands for the car's actuators like the steering system, the throttle, and the brakes.

4.5. Benefits and Challenges of Autonomous Driving

The benefits of autonomous vehicles can be profound. They hold the promise of substantially reducing traffic accidents caused by human error, improving traffic flow and reducing congestion, and significantly lowering CO_2 emissions.

However, there are still many hurdles to cross, primarily technical and regulatory. AI models must be extensively trained and validated to operate safely in various scenarios and conditions. Also, regulations and standards need to be put into place to ensure the safe operation of these technologies on public roads.

Simultaneously, ethical questions concerning responsibility and decision-making in critical situations must be addressed. As we inch closer to a world where cars drive themselves, grappling with these challenges will be crucial.

4.6. Conclusion

In conclusion, the incorporation of AI within the realm of the automotive industry and its associated offshoots is not a trope of futuristic fantasy but a tangible reality we are witnessing unfold today. The ever-improving ability of AI to amalgamate the tangible—that which we can touch—with the intangible—that which we can but imagine—is shaping up to be one of the greatest technological revolutions in human history.

In the not-so-distant future, AI-powered automatic and assisted driving may not just be a luxury or a novelty but an integrated part of the transportation system. Deep-seated transformation comes with its own share of benefits and challenges, but it is vital to recognize that they echo the continued progress of technological evolution. What we require is a comprehensive blend of curiosity, innovation, adaptation, and regulation as we continue this riveting journey along the highway of progress.

Chapter 5. The Power of Predictive Maintenance: AI's Proactive Approach

Predictive maintenance has been a long-standing pursuit in the automotive industry, and with the advent of artificial intelligence, it has been elevated to a new dimension. This technique utilizes machine learning algorithms to forecast potential equipment failures or faults, materializing before they have caused harm or ceased operation entirely. It revolutionizes the relationship between drivers, their vehicles, and their safety.

5.1. AI: Predictive Maintenance's Gateway

To understand the role of artificial intelligence in predictive maintenance, it's necessary first to underline what predictive maintenance is. Generally speaking, predictive maintenance is a proactive approach that seeks to foresee possible machine malfunctions and arrange for necessary upkeep and repairs gradually and in a well-timed manner, well before failure eventually occurs. AI invigorates this process by delivering on the promise to predict failures accurately and in real-time.

By implementing machine learning protocols, AI can amass historical data, analyze patterns, and accurately pinpoint the imminent issues. The potency of this combination increases as it continues learning, improving with each round of analysis and prediction. This efficient and cost-effective cycle represents a significant advantage for automotive proprietors, minimizing both time spent diagnosing issues and the financial burden.

5.2. Need for Predictive Maintenance

It's essential to appreciate why predictive maintenance is so critical for the automotive industry. It reducing the chances of catastrophic breakdowns, decreases maintenance costs, extends equipment lives, and minimizes downtime associated with unexpected repairs.

The costs for unscheduled repairs, often resulting from sudden equipment failure, can be exorbitant. Not only do they require immediate and often costly attention but they also cause lost productivity and potentially compromised safety. With the predictive maintenance approach, these repairs can be scheduled, perhaps bundled with other routine services, and executed in a more cost-effective approach.

5.3. AI Applications in Predictive Maintenance

AI provides two primary values in predictive maintenance: anomaly detection and failure prediction. Anomaly detection identifies rare or suspicious data points that deviate from normal behavior, often due to an irregularity in the machine. On the other hand, failure prediction assesses the future risk of failure based on existing data.

Given the dramatic increase of sensors and data collection devices embedded in modern vehicles, AI has a wider scope in identifying and diagnosing impending faults and failures. For instance, anomalous vibrations in a car might signify a looming engine failure. AI systems can identify this pattern and prepare an alert. Advanced algorithms can measure and analyze this vibration in real time, comparing the results to historical vibration patterns. By recognizing a pattern or an anomaly, AI can predict an impending failure in the engine and deploy an alert for preventive action to be taken.

5.4. The Future of AI in Predictive Maintenance

As the implementation of AI in the automotive industry progresses, the impact on predictive maintenance will become more pronounced. The convergence of the Internet of Things (IoT), machine learning, and deep learning models will create a robust framework for the cognitive predictive maintenance model.

Cloud-based AI models will serve as the backbone of this framework, where large volumes of sensor data can be processed, stored, and analyzed. Data from different models, brands, and types of cars will feed into the predictive maintenance machine learning models increasing their accuracy and efficiency.

Under this model, cars will communicate directly with service centers, alerting them about upcoming needed maintenance. Service providers can then schedule appointments timely before problematic issues arise, ensuring a smoother, more effortless maintenance process. Thus, the future of AI in predictive maintenance envisages a paradigm where vehicles self-diagnose, communicate to the humans about their health status, and suggest informed choices for their upkeep.

The harmonization of artificial intelligence with predictive maintenance in the automotive industry sets a high threshold. Still, as vehicles continue to modernize and become more tightly interwoven with technology, the potential for groundbreaking innovation becomes more palpable.

To close, we may argue that beyond just providing a luxurious, cutting-edge driving experience, the ultimate objective of AI in predictive maintenance is to ensure safety, improve economy, decrease downtime, and deliver peace of mind to the car proprietors and operators. As we continue to dive into an era where data and machine learning fuels our progression, these objectives will only become more attainable and the voyage even more effortless.

Chapter 6. Car Connectivity and AI: Envisioning The Internet of Vehicles

The arrival of sophisticated technology has led to a dramatic change in cars, transforming them into more than just a transportation tool. Today, vehicles can diagnose their mechanical issues, recommend the fastest routes, and even drive themselves. Central to this transformation is the accelerated adoption of Artificial Intelligence (AI) and the rise of the Internet of Vehicles (IoV).

6.1. AI and IoT in Connected Vehicles

Artificial Intelligence (AI) and the Internet of Things (IoT), when applied together in vehicles, offer a multitude of advantages. Connected vehicles use IoT devices to gather, analyze, and act upon data to improve overall performance while AI provides the intelligence needed to make sense of this data, automate tasks, and enhance driving experiences.

Modern cars connect with other IoT devices, such as traffic lights, smart city infrastructure, and other vehicles, making driving safer and more efficient. AI algorithms facilitate these connections by analyzing traffic congestion patterns to devise the most efficient routes or recognizing the signs of mechanical failure in the vehicle before causing any significant damage.

6.2. Adopting Deep Learning Techniques

Deep Learning, a subset of AI, has become an essential tool in connected vehicles, aiding in the interpretation and utilization of vast amounts of data. These neural networks model the human brain's functioning to recognize patterns and make sense of complex, unstructured data.

Applications of Deep Learning in vehicles are manifold, including real-time object detection, predictive maintenance, and improved mapping and routing. For instance, traffic sign interpretation uses Deep Learning to categorize different traffic signs and react accordingly, thus ensuring safe and law-abiding driving.

6.3. Ensuring Vehicle Security

As vehicles become more networked, they also become vulnerable to cyber threats. Thus, AI-driven security protocols are critical in ensuring the safety and security of connected vehicles. Machine Learning (ML) algorithms can identify and respond to potential hacks or intrusions by learning from previous cyber-attacks. Additionally, AI can help detect abnormal vehicle behavior, which could indicate a mechanical or system failure.

6.4. The Future: Autonomous and Self-driving Cars

The future of the automotive industry lies in autonomous vehicles, and AI plays a pivotal role in this evolution. It helps in areas such as sensor fusion, localization, path planning, and control. Autopilots in Tesla's innovative cars serve as the best instance of AI's role in enabling autonomous driving, where advanced sensors and algorithms work together to navigate the car.

Self-driving cars will rely extensively on data—data from the car's sensors, historical driving data, and real-time traffic data. With the help of AI, these self-contained ecosystems will process information and make well-informed decisions.

6.5. Standardizing AI Across the Auto Industry

As industries move towards vehicle connectivity, setting a standardized protocol for AI becomes vital. Standardizing AI in automobiles will ensure the technology's seamless application, regardless of the manufacturer. It guarantees that the same quality and safety principles apply, ensuring that all vehicles operate within the same criteria and uphold the same performance and safety standards.

6.6. Economic and Environmental Impact of AI in Cars

The impact of AI-driven cars will extend beyond technology, with significant economic and environmental implications. AI can lead to transport services' democratization, opening new business avenues and reducing costs. On the environmental side, AI can promote greener practices through optimized routing and fuel management, reducing the carbon footprints of vehicles.

Artificial Intelligence is undoubtedly remolding the automotive industry. Its impact, while impressive today, promises only to grow with the advent of self-driving cars and more advanced machine learning techniques. This leap in AI and vehicle connectivity is setting a new direction for the sector. The Internet of Vehicles is no longer a conceptual notion but a tangible reality that is gradually coming to life. This fascinating interplay between vehicles, AI, and connectivity is transforming the way we view and use our cars and potentially even how our cities operate.

Chapter 7. Artificial Intelligence and Electric Vehicles: A Dynamic Duo

While it is often viewed as a singular realm, the automotive industry is a multifaceted domain with distinct yet intertwined segments. One of these rapidly evolving segments pertains to electric vehicles. The advent of AI into this domain has triggered a paradigm shift, setting in motion a dynamic duo that can fundamentally alter our transportation landscape.

7.1. Rise of Electric Vehicles

The increase in strict environmental regulations, emphasis on reducing carbon emissions and technological advancements have fostered the growth of electric vehicles (EVs). A KPMG report forecasts that EVs are likely to represent 30% of the global vehicle market share by 2030. The electrification of cars doesn't only entail swapping an internal combustion engine for an electric motor but also invites a host of other revolutionary changes such as novel energy management systems, evolving driver-car interfaces, and new vehicle designs. In all of these domains, artificial intelligence emerges as a crucial player.

7.2. AI at the Heart of EVs

The incorporation of AI supports several aspects of an electric vehicle's functionality. From autonomous driving, predictive maintenance, to optimal energy management, AI breathes life into the potential of EVs. Implicit in the successful operation of these systems is the use of complex algorithms that analyze large data sets in real-time, enabling these functions.

7.3. Autonomous Driving

Autonomous driving is a conspicuous AI application in electric vehicles. AI-powered sensors and cameras are fused to create a real-time, 360-degree view of the surroundings. Machine learning algorithms then process this data to understand the environment and predict possible changes. Decision-making algorithms finally provide the necessary instructions to the vehicle to adjust its speed, direction or to activate other systems as required.

A noteworthy example of this is Tesla's Autopilot system which is continually improved via over-the-air software updates. The system gains data from Tesla's fleet learning, where vehicles independently gather data when Autopilot is activated, continually fortifying the algorithms.

7.4. Predictive Maintenance

In predictive maintenance, AI algorithms predict the likelihood of an impending failure in components or the system. The early identification and subsequent rectification of these issues can prevent costly repairs, improve the vehicle's lifetime, and enhance user safety. AI-based predictive maintenance solutions evaluate historical data, along with real-time information from sensors integrated into various vehicle components, to make these predictions. Companies like SparkCognition and Predii offer AI-led predictive maintenance solutions for the automotive industry.

7.5. Optimal Energy Management

A pivotal concern for every EV owner is mileage or 'range anxiety'. AI can play a considerable role in alleviating this anxiety. AI algorithms can manage energy consumption based on the topography of the routes, the traffic conditions, utilization of in-car systems, driving behavior, and weather conditions. Google's DeepMind has demonstrated how AI can reduce energy use recently by optimizing cooling in data centers, and these principles can be extended to improve the energy efficiency of EVs.

7.6. User Experience

AI opens the door for bespoke user experiences by adapting to the individual preferences of drivers in an EV. Gestures, voice commands, and even the driver's emotions and health condition can be discerned by AI to customize the driving or riding experience. Companies such as Affectiva and Eyeris use emotion recognition AI to inform the vehicle if the driver is distracted or drowsy, enhancing safety.

7.7. AI and EVs: Challenges and Prospects

While AI brings numerous advantages and possibilities, there are still significant challenges to confront. Issues relating to cybersecurity, privacy, and the ethical guidelines for autonomous driving stand among them. As EVs are poised to be data centers on wheels, robust encryption and security measures must be in place. Standards and regulations need to keep pace with the rapid development of this technology.

In spite of these challenges, AI and EVs form a symbiotic relationship combining sustainable transportation with cutting-edge technology. As huge strides are made in AI, the next generation of energy-efficient, self-driving, AI-powered electric vehicles can be expected to be transformative, heralding a new era in the automotive industry. The swift adoption of this dynamic duo by automotive manufacturers manifests the long, exciting journey that we are set to embark on in the realm of transportation.

Chapter 8. Improving Safety Measures through AI: Advanced Driver-Assistance Systems

Once predominantly under the purview of science fiction, AI's convergence with the automotive industry is now a reality, transforming not only how we drive but crucially, elevating safety measures through innovations such as Advanced Driver-Assistance Systems (ADAS). This manifold marriage of AI and automotive technologies attributes to a safer, more intuitive, and efficient driving environment.

8.1. Understanding ADAS

ADAS is a set of systems that assist drivers in their driving and parking process, aiming to bolster vehicular safety and overall convenience. It encompasses numerous features, including automated lighting, predicting pedestrians, automatic braking, GPS traffic warnings, connectivity, and more. These systems utilize a range of technology including LiDAR, radar, cameras, ultrasonic sensors, and AI.

To appreciate the magnitude of ADAS's impact and its relation to AI, it's essential to consider its individual components and interconnected technologies.

8.2. Adaptive Cruise Control

Adaptive Cruise Control (ACC) is one of the earliest ADAS technologies, where an integrated radar and a camera setup dynamically adjusts the vehicle's speed to maintain a safe driving distance from other vehicles. With AI, the ACC system can accurately predict the behaviors of nearby drivers and make real-time adjustments accordingly.

8.3. Automatic Emergency Braking

At the forefront of ADAS's safety agenda, Automatic Emergency Braking (AEB) uses sensors to detect potential collision objects, alerts the driver, and will automatically apply the brakes if the driver fails to respond promptly.

8.4. Lane-keeping Assist

Lane-keeping Assist (LKA), another standout ADAS feature, uses AI to process real-time camera data and detect lane markings on the road. Via these findings, the system can help drivers stay in their lane or perform safe lane changes when the indicators are used.

8.5. Blind Spot Detection

The potentially life-saving function of Blind Spot Detection illustrates how radar sensors and AI algorithms combine to warn drivers of vehicles in their blind spots when changing lanes.

8.6. Intelligent Parking

No longer considered an upscale feature, intelligent parking systems are now a mainstream element in a broad array of car models. The AI guides the vehicle into a parking space with minimal input from the driver.

8.7. AI and Model Simulation

Advanced AI models can simulate myriad complex scenarios to train ADAS, making it more adaptive and robust. Through these simulations, AI models can strategize against potential hazards, thus reducing chances of collisions and enhancing overall traffic safety.

8.8. AI-Powered Predictive Maintenance

AI not only assists in the active operation of a vehicle but also aids in its maintenance. Predictive maintenance, powered by AI, employs machine learning algorithms for early fault detection in systems and components.

8.9. Enhanced Connectivity and V2X Communication

V2X(Vehicle-To-Everything) communication empowers smart cars to communicate with 'everything'—including smart infrastructure, other vehicles, and pedestrian devices. It enhances the safety of the vehicle and its passengers by predicting potential risks ahead.

While incorporating AI into ADAS significantly improves vehicular safety, it's critical to acknowledge and mitigate potential challenges.

8.10. Challenges and Roadblocks

AI in the automotive industry is not without its challenges. Data security and privacy concerns loom large. Creating foolproof AI models remains a formidable task, given the complexity of real-world driving conditions. False positives and false negatives can also lead to hazardous driving situations.

Despite these challenges, AI's promise in redefining safety mechanisms in vehicles is undeniably transformative. As ADAS technologies continue to evolve with AI, it will revolutionize the future of driving, making it safer, more efficient, and more convenient. One thing is clear: The road ahead for AI in ADAS looks promising, paving the way for a new era in the automotive industry.

Chapter 9. AI's Role in Supply Chain and Production

Artificial Intelligence (AI) is revolutionizing the automotive industry's supply chain and production procedures. Chronicled here are the facets of this development.

9.1. Impact of AI on Supply Chain Management

Within the automotive industry, managing supply chains can be complex due to intricate networks of suppliers, manufacturers, and consumers. AI's role, therefore, offers valuable opportunities to streamline these processes.

Predictive analysis enables businesses to forecast demand and manage supply efficiently. Machine Learning models can analyze historical sales data, promotional schedules, geographical location, and other factors to provide accurate predictions. The ability to anticipate demand fluctuations allows businesses to adjust their production schedules, thereby avoiding surplus or scarcity scenarios, reducing costs, and enhancing customer satisfaction.

AI can also foster collaboration between various supply chain partners through improved information sharing. By integrating AI technologies, businesses can ensure seamless data access, transparency, and real-time tracking of processes. For instance, blockchain technology offers an immutable record of each transaction and change in the supply chain, providing total visibility.

Moreover, AI enhances risk management in supply chain operations. By feeding data about incidents (like supplier failures, quality issues, or geopolitical events) into predictive models, businesses can foresee potential disruptions. This proactive approach allows them to devise contingency plans, minimizing the impact of any disturbances.

9.2. Incorporation of AI in Manufacturing

AI's imprint on manufacturing is delineated through advanced robotics, smart factories, and quality control advancements.

Advanced robotics deployed in factories are far more sophisticated than their predecessors, attributed mainly to AI. Enabled with features like visual recognition and advanced sensor technology, these self-learning robots can perform complex tasks with better efficiency, meanwhile reducing hazardous labor.

Smart factories represent another key contribution of AI. Utilizing IOT devices and AI technologies, such factories provide an integrated, interconnected manufacturing environment. This setup provides real-time insights into operations, enables predictive maintenance (identifying machine faults before they cause breakdowns), and fosters efficient energy management.

In terms of quality control, AI can be a significant asset. Machine vision systems can scrutinize products more accurately and consistently than human inspectors, detecting defects in real-time, and reducing errors. These systems can be trained through Deep Learning models to recognize a wide variety of defects, even those unseen by the human eye.

9.3. AI for Customized Production

Tradition dictates that cars are produced en masse with predetermined features. However, the new era beckons personalized production, and AI catalyzes this shift. Using AI, manufacturers can process customer data quicker, identifying trends, and accommodating individual preferences in the production line. This strategy allows for delivering vehicles more in alignment with customer expectations, enhancing their satisfaction, and increasing brand loyalty.

Furthermore, 3D printing technology, coupled with AI software, supports the production of custom parts. This combination optimizes costs, as manufacturing such elements conventionally can be expensive and lead to excess waste.

9.4. The Roadmap to Future

AI undoubtedly offers significant advantages to automotive supply chain and production, but the journey is not without challenges. These encompass security concerns, data management issues, and the requisite for substantial investments. Therefore, companies must equip themselves to navigate these journeys.

In essence, AI's role in automobile supply chain and production furnishes promising prospects. Its capacity to streamline operations, promote collaboration, augment quality control, and enable personalized production advocates robust growth potential for the industry. Given its myriad benefits, it is certain that businesses will increasingly pursue AI applications to refine their supply chain and production processes in the future.

Nevertheless, considering the infancy of this shift, continuous research, exploration, and appropriate regulatory measures will be vital to fully harness AI's potential within the automotive realm. We stand on the brink of a profound evolution, a juncture where artificial intelligence is poised to revolutionize how we produce and deliver the vehicles of tomorrow.

Chapter 10. Addressing Ethical and Legal Concerns: Autonomy and Accountability in AI Adoption

The adoption of artificial intelligence in the automotive industry brings about monumental changes, but with this innovation comes various challenges encompassing ethical and legal spectrums. In this context, particularly with autonomous vehicles, two major concerns – autonomy and accountability – come to the fore.

10.1. Understanding Autonomy in Autonomous Vehicles

AI-powered vehicles are equipped with the power of autonomy, meaning they hold the capacity to navigate and operate without human intervention. This concept of vehicle autonomy can be further elucidated into five levels depending on human involvement:

- Level 0: This is the base level where all the car operations are controlled manually.

- Level 1: Some vehicle systems, like cruise control and automatic braking, can be controlled autonomously.

- Level 2: The vehicle has partial automation, which means it can control both steering and acceleration/deceleration.

- Level 3: The vehicle becomes conditionally autonomous, where it can manage most aspects of driving, but human override is needed when the system cannot handle the situation.

- Level 4: The vehicle becomes highly autonomous and can operate without human interaction in most circumstances, but the manual override option remains.

- Level 5: This is the topmost level where the vehicle is fully autonomous and requires no human intervention.

Advancements in AI technology fuel the shift from lower to higher levels of autonomy. However, the higher the autonomy, the more complex the ethical challenges become.

10.2. Ethical Dilemmas in Autonomous Vehicles

Autonomous vehicles need to make split-second decisions, and these decisions may sometimes pose grave ethical dilemmas. For instance, there may be situations where a collision is inevitable, but the vehicle must decide where to direct the impact – towards pedestrians or towards the car occupants.

To resolve such dilemmas, ethics for AI-powered vehicles must be defined. While some suggest that the ethics of AI should be guided by utilitarian principles, which prioritize actions leading to the highest overall good, others propose a deontological approach, where certain principles are held as universally binding. Striking a balance in such situations remains a major challenge.

10.3. Legal Concerns With Autonomous Vehicles

Legal systems worldwide are designed around the concept that a human is always at the driver's seat. As autonomous cars step in, the question arises: who should be accountable if an accident occurs? Is it the owner, the manufacturer, or the AI itself?

The Vienna Convention on Road Traffic – an international treaty designed to facilitate international road traffic and increase road safety – states that every vehicle in traffic must have a driver, and the driver is always responsible for control over their vehicle. The rise of self-driving cars challenges this principle on international law. Will these laws need to be amended in the light of AI-driven vehicles?

10.4. Liability and Insurance

While determining the accountability in cases of accidents involving autonomous vehicles may be complex, insurance companies also face a consequential quandary. With fewer accidents, premiums may decrease. However, when accidents do occur, the costs can be significantly higher due to the expensive technology embedded in these vehicles. Who will bear these costs?

Further, manufacturers may be forced to accept the liability for the actions of AI-controlled vehicles, entirely flipping the current fault-based model on its head. It's a massive shift that would require a complete overhaul of the laws regulating vehicular transportation. Companies would potentially be incentivized to invest massive amounts in safety to minimize their liability.

10.5. Privacy Issues

Connected vehicles that use AI rely on extensive data collection about the vehicle's surroundings and the users themselves. This presents a wealth of useful information for infotainment, navigation, and safety purposes.

However, these data can also be used for nefarious purposes if they fall into the wrong hands. Without proper legal and ethical frameworks for data collection, privacy, and security, this could be a potential risk. In many parts of the world, there are no comprehensive regulations yet regarding who has access, who owns data, and how it can be used and protected.

Navigating through these legal and ethical quandaries requires an objective understanding of the technology, along with foresight and planning, to steer the course of autonomous vehicles towards a safe and protected future. The promising benefits of autonomous cars, such as fewer accidents, increased mobility, reduced emissions, and more, hinge upon successfully addressing these ethical and legal concerns.

Chapter 11. The Road Ahead: Predictions and Possibilities for AI in Automotive

Artificial intelligence (AI) has been making inroads into the automotive industry, transforming everything from manufacturing to self-driving technology. Let's unpack the various predictions and possibilities around AI's integration in the automotive world.

11.1. Breakthroughs in Autonomous Vehicles

One of the most anticipated applications of AI in the domain of automobiles is in the arena of autonomous or self-driving vehicles. Autonomous vehicles rely heavily on AI to scan and interpret their surroundings, implement machine learning for decision-making, and auto-pilot the vehicle safety and effectively.

Consider the example of Tesla, which now promises Full Self-Driving (FSD) capabilities for complete automation. Vital in these breakthroughs are the AI algorithms that power Tesla's Autopilot software. These algorithms assimilate data from the car's many sensors and make millions of calculations every second to keep the vehicle on the road and ensure the safety of its passengers.

Other notable players like Waymo, Google's self-driving car project, and Uber's Advanced Technologies Group, are also making substantial progress in autonomous vehicles using AI.

Exactly how soon fully autonomous vehicles will become commonplace on our streets is debatable. According to estimates by the Boston Consulting Group, by 2035, one-quarter of miles driven in the US could be through shared, self-driving vehicles.

11.2. Enhancing Automotive Manufacturing

Artificial Intelligence has the potential to revolutionize vehicle manufacturing. Manufacturers all over the globe are applying AI in their production lines to increase efficiency, improve safety, and deliver higher quality vehicles.

For instance, AI can supervise and manage the parts inventory to optimize resources and prevent delays in the production line. Besides, AI-powered robots can assist workers with heavy lifting or dangerous tasks. AI can also aid in understanding and predicting faults in the production line, enabling preemptive maintenance and reducing downtime.

11.3. Intelligent Traffic Management Systems

As AI begins to play a more prominent role in the transport infrastructure, intelligent traffic management systems are set to become a reality. These systems would use AI to analyze traffic patterns, predict congestion, and adjust signals in real time to optimize the flow of traffic.

Countries like Singapore are already testing AI technology to manage their traffic conditions. Their system uses AI to monitor traffic and weather conditions to predict and prevent potential road incidents. The system can then guide emergency services to the location even before the incident occurs. The concept can also be extended to manage smart parking solutions, predict road maintenance needs, and more.

11.4. Personalized Driving Experience

Modern cars are becoming increasingly connected. As a result, they can gather vast quantities of data about the driving habits and preferences of the user. AI is poised to utilize this data to offer a highly personalized driving experience.

In-car AI systems can learn preferences like preferred route, music preferences, frequent destinations, and so forth. These systems could also provide personalized reminders for car maintenance, payments, or appointments.

11.5. Cybersecurity and AI

As automobiles become more connected, they also become more exposed to potential cyber attacks. Cybersecurity is a growing concern in the automotive industry, and AI can come to the rescue.

AI has the potential to continuously monitor for suspicious activities, identify potential threats, and take precautionary actions in real time. Moreover, AI can learn from past incidents to predict and prevent future attacks.

To wrap up, the AI revolution in the automotive industry is just getting started. If the staggering pace of advancement continues, our relationship with vehicles and how we move around will undergo a total transformation within a few decades. However, it is important to monitor these developments closely and take steps to navigate potential obstacles such as data privacy issues, ethical considerations, and the need for appropriate legal and regulatory frameworks.